CW00558262

The Real Jack Ryan

FORMER CIA ANALYST TELLS THE REAL LIFE
STORY OF THE US GOVERNMENT'S TOP SECRET
SPY AGENCY

Scott Schlimmer

I bit into a hamburger. Grease dripped onto a sheet of paper. This was no ordinary piece of paper. It was TOP SECRET.

This was my first time seeing a TOP SECRET document, which should have been a momentous occasion. But we were in the middle of a crisis simulation, and there's no time for a lunch break during a crisis! So, my first TOP SECRET document doubled as a grease napkin. A bit anti-climactic.

This combination of state secrets and burger grease perfectly summarizes my experience as a CIA analyst. As The Real Jack Ryan.

Jack Ryan, famously, is Tom Clancy's character who is a CIA analyst and is asked to do missions more akin to James Bond. Jack Ryan first appears in The Hunt for Red October and in many other movies and TV series. Jack Ryan has been played by Alec Baldwin, Harrison Ford, Ben Affleck, Chris Pine, and John Krasinski.

As you might imagine, Hollywood's Jack Ryan could not be further from reality. The real life of a CIA analyst is a little more like The Office, which ironically would make John Krasinski perfect. I found the job to be a bizarre combination of fascinating CIA adventures and comical government bureaucracy. The Real Jack Ryan is more heartwarming and funny, but with fewer near-death situations and car chases.

Unfortunately, this reality is not portrayed accurately by Hollywood.

In this book, you'll learn the reality, firsthand, from someone who was a real CIA analyst. Unlike the movies, everything in this book is true. Nothing has been made up, fabricated, or embellished. Only some names have been changed, as current and former CIA officers often appreciate their anonymity.

This real story includes things like:

> -My background and path to the CIA, like my first contact with The CIA at...a Career Fair, of all places.

> -The reality of the job: from exciting things like advising the President to mundane staff meetings.

> -Some bizarre and interesting stories that could only happen to CIA analysts, like telling Stevie Wonder about when I heard someone sing his songs in Tajikistan.

> -And finally, the answers to the questions I'm most often asked. Most likely these are the questions you would ask if you sat down to have a beer with a CIA analyst.

I personally think the reality is more interesting than the Hollywood mythology. You truly can't make this stuff up!

Read on and decide for yourself.

-Scott Schlimmer
Former CIA analyst & The Real Jack Ryan

The Real Jack Ryan at CIA Headquarters at Langley.

TABLE OF CONTENTS

THE CIA "DOES NOT OBJECT TO THIS BOOK."
(AND OTHER CIA DISCLAIMERS)

First, we need to start with the disclaimers. The CIA asked me to tell you this: (seriously)

> "All statements of fact, opinion, or analysis expressed are those of the author and do not reflect the official positions or views of the U.S. Government. Nothing in the contents should be construed as asserting or implying U.S. Government authentication of information or endorsement of the author's views."

Ok, "asked" isn't exactly the right word. They told me I had to do it!

But the statement is true. I wrote everything in this book. The CIA and US Government's only contribution was to redact and delete things.

For background, I had to send this book to the CIA's Prepublication Classification Review Board (PCRB) for review. The review took 20 days.

Here are some highlights from that review:

> "PCRB determined that it [your book] contains classified information that must be removed before sharing or publishing. We have attached a partial copy of your work showing the affected text marked for deletion. These changes are not optional — they are mandatory, and the work should not be shared with anyone until the changes are made."

Ouch, ok. No blurred lines, there.

> "Once you have removed/altered the classified material as shown in the attached copy and added the disclaimer, PCRB will have no further objection to its publication."

So there you go, the CIA "has no further objections to this book." That's the CIA's equivalent of "Two Thumbs Up" from Siskel & Ebert, right?
(Author's note: To make sure I don't end up in jail, I should clarify that no, it isn't.)

How that we've got the disclaimers out of the way, let's get to the juicy stuff. Or at least all the juicy stuff I was allowed to publish! (don't worry, there's plenty)

SCOTT SCHLIMMER

CHAPTER 1

PATH TO THE CIA, MY FORMATIVE YEARS

People often wonder, how does someone end up working at the CIA? Does the government groom them from birth to be special agents? Do they spend their whole lives preparing for CIA life?

The short answer...no.

I'm often asked about the early details of my life, which I personally would have thought would bore everyone but my Mom. But since I'm so often asked, I probably should include it in this book.

If you're not interested in my background and want to learn more about the realities of being a CIA analyst, don't hesitate to skip ahead. I won't be offended!

This book is designed so that each story stands on its own. You can jump around to whichever topics you find most interesting.

Here are some highlights you'll find in this chapter.

1: What were you like as a child?

2: Nerd or popular? (a.k.a analyst or spy)

3: Did all paths lead to Langley?

1: WHAT WERE YOU LIKE AS A CHILD?

I was a bit of a nerd, as a child. My friends and I loved video games, and we played Super Nintendo for hours. During the summer, my parents would push us to go outside. Maybe go to the beach, which now I'd love to do. But we just wanted to stay inside and play video games.

> "I scored high on aptitude tests from a
> young age – usually in the top 1%."

I was always a smart kid. I scored high on aptitude tests from a young age – usually in the top 1%. But it was never a big deal to me. While I found myself in some accelerated and gifted programs, I mostly lived like a normal kid, taking normal classes, living the normal life.

We weren't especially wealthy, and could even be called lower-middle income. We weren't ever poor, but my parents dropped out of college when I was born (although I don't think they were spending much time in the library before I was born!) and they both worked hard to pay the rent, keep food on the table, and provide me with a comfortable life.

For whatever we lacked in money, I had great parents who were extremely devoted and made up for it with parenting and love. Both wanted me to live a more privileged life than they had lived, and they worked hard to give me every opportunity and taught me why I wanted to make the most of them.

My parents were the type to work overtime and cut spending so I could go on the class trip. Or to pay for my sports equipment so I could be on the baseball team. But there was no way they were going to let me miss either experience. When they divorced, each remarried to amazing step-parents, who were both wonderful and treated me like their own child. I consider myself extremely lucky on the parental front.

The Real Jack Ryan when he was a dashing young boy.

2: NERD OR POPULAR? (A.K.A ANALYST OR SPY)

Speaking of nerdiness and sports equipment, which one was I? Was I the geeky kid or the popular athlete?

Undoubtedly at CIA, the Jack Ryan-esque analysts are the geeks. And the "spies" are the popular kids.
(Authors Note: They are not actually called spies; they are called Case Officers or Operations Officers. However, I'll use "spies" to denote Case Officers or Operations Officers because so many people will be more familiar with the term.)

So which am I? Nerd or popular? I'm kind of both, actually. I split the difference.

> "I decided to quit the Varsity basketball team to join the Quiz Bowl team."

One story that sums it up well: I had made the Varsity Basketball team as a Junior in high school. And this was a bad basketball team that hardly ever won. And still, I never got any playing time. Instead of sitting on the bench watching my team lose, I decided to quit the basketball team to join the Quiz Bowl team.

It doesn't get any geekier than Quiz Bowl. Quiz Bowl is like Jeopardy, but you play on a team against other schools. That means I have the dubious distinction of quitting the Varsity Basketball team to join the Quiz Bowl team. Ladies, don't all call at once.

So, I definitely got along with the geeks, smart kids, and nerds. A.k.a the CIA analysts of the school yard.

But I was also a pretty good athlete, and that made me friends among the jocks and the "cool kids." A.k.a the CIA "spies" of the school yard.

I made the Varsity Baseball team as a Freshman, and ended up being an All Conference baseball player who helped lead my team to the conference championship my Senior Year. I actually still play baseball, to this day. (But not softball!)

I was fast and a pretty good runner. After setting the Middle School Tri County Conference record for the 70-yard dash, I ended up becoming a distance runner and joining the Cross Country team. To be honest, I joined the Cross Country team because one of my best friends was the best runner in my school's history and asked me to join, too, with him. And, it didn't hurt that as a 14 year old boy, I saw during the first practice that gorgeous, athletic 18-year old "women" were running around wearing sports bras. That was all the convincing I needed!

But in the end, I finished as an All Conference and All Region runner who won many conference championships and also won countless awards and medals. To give you a sense, my one mile time was 5 minutes (although Cross Country is a 5 km sport).

So, I was an odd combination of both nerdy and popular. A bit CIA analyst and a bit CIA "Spy". But in the end, CIA analyst was the better fit for me.

The Real Jack Ryan's quiz bowl team huddles up. Definitely an element of nerdy/analyst!

3: DID ALL PATHS LEAD TO LANGLEY?

Many people think that people who end up at CIA plan to be CIA officers their whole lives, and that all of life leading up to the job is done with the goal of ending up in Langley.

For me, this could not be further from the truth. I never envisioned myself working at the CIA.

> "I never envisioned myself working at the CIA."

I did study political science in college, which is a natural fit for a CIA analyst. A student of politics is well-positioned to analyze a foreign nation's politics. But I studied American political science. International politics would be a more proper fit for a job with the CIA.

I did an internship with a foreign government during college. I worked with the Canadian House of Commons in Ottawa for a summer. Keep in mind that Ottawa is a 1-hour drive from the US border.

I learned a lot about foreign governments while

working with Canada, however, and how they viewed the United States. And I used that knowledge when I joined the CIA to analyze foreign governments.

But I was 19. The real reason I chose the internship was because you can legally drink at age 19 in Canada. And drink I did! My main memory of my internship was when the Canadian beer companies lobbied us, with plenty of free samples.

I was also involved in government-like things. My freshman year I was elected Treasurer of the University of Michigan's Mary Markley Hall, my dorm/residence hall. This meant I managed the budget for fun events. And my sophomore year I was elected Vice President of Records for the Residence Halls Association, the student government body presiding over all the dorms/residence halls at the university.

The Real Jack Ryan in college at a student government meeting.

I also saw myself as an English minor, and I took a lot of writing classes. This turned out to be important because writing is a major part of the CIA analyst's work. We often wrote for the President of the United States, Congressmen, and top government leaders.

> "But most importantly, I was just a smart, talented generalist. I gained a lot of important skills that could be applied to any challenge. And this is the main reason CIA chose me."

But most importantly, I was just a smart, talented generalist. I gained a lot of important skills that could be applied to any challenge. And this is the main reason CIA chose me. CIA hires two types of people to be analysts: one is a subject matter expert who has become an expert about a country or a topic. They may have visited the country or region, speak the language, and studied its history and current events. That's not me, unless you count Canada! The other type of person is the generalist, who can be placed on topics for which there aren't enough experts, yet, perhaps because the topic is new and difficult. I was very much the latter.

I also saw myself as a lawyer, and I intended to go to law school. I took the LSAT, the intense entrance exam for law school. And I didn't do well. This, along with a book I was reading at the time, Scott Turow's One L, dissuaded me from law school. I thought, if doing poorly on one test is enough to hamper a career in law and prevent me from attending a top law school, then maybe it's not the field for me. And, perhaps more importantly, I couldn't find a lawyer who actually enjoyed their job.

That left me in the precarious position of, "Well, what do I do, now?" I ultimately pursued a Master's Degree in Public Policy, also at the University of Michigan. This program focused heavily on policy analysis and was an amazing program. But again, I focused on domestic policy, not international policy. Still, it was great preparation for analyzing foreign governments, and the program consistently ranks Top 5 in the country for public policy analysis.

It was during graduate school that I made my first contact with the CIA. The next chapter focuses on these first contacts. So, read on if you'd like to know more!

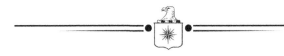

Chapter 2

Getting The Job & First Interactions With The Agency

How does one even get a job with the CIA? This chapter dives into the long, arduous process of getting a job as a CIA analyst. It starts with the application process and interviews, and then everything that is required to get Top Secret clearance.

Here are some highlights you'll find in this chapter.

4: First contact with the CIA…at a career fair?!

5: How does one get an analyst job at the CIA?

6: The security clearance investigation

7: Medical examination & the dreaded polygraph

8: What's the first thing to do after receiving a security clearance? Get a raise!

4: First contact with the CIA…at a career fair?!

It all started at a career fair. Yes, a career fair. I know, no CIA movie starts at a career fair. But mine is a different kind of story. It's a real story, for starters. Like real life, parts of it are mundane.

And parts of life at CIA were mundane. But also, because it was the CIA, parts of it were like a movie.

Stacey—my girlfriend at the time who lived with me at the University of Michigan—mentioned wanting to go to a career fair to talk with people representing the US Government agency Health and Human Services. That didn't interest me, but I saw that ESPN would be at the career fair. I was a 24 year old guy, about to finish grad school who didn't know what I wanted to do in life. A chat with ESPN and a chance to support my shy girlfriend was enough for me.

I printed a few resumes, dusted off the old suit, and headed to the career fair. In the end, ESPN didn't wow me, but there was a CIA booth not too far from ESPN.

"ESPN didn't wow me, but there was a CIA booth not too far from ESPN at the career fair."

Yes, it is as odd as it sounds. CIA has a booth at a career fair.

I wasn't recruited in a dark alley or a hotel room. But I walked up to the CIA booth at the career fair, and I said hello to a friendly looking man. Little did I know, he was Peter C., one of the top officials in the Directorate of Intelligence—CIA's analysis division (which is now called the DA-Directorate of Analysis). As you might expect, his description of the CIA sold me hook, line, and sinker.

Ultimately, I decided to apply to the CIA simply because it sounded like a really cool job.
(Side note: Stacey ultimately did work for Health and Human Services, many years later)

A screenshot from a virtual CIA career fair.
Much more elegant than the career fair where I went to!

5: HOW DOES ONE GET AN ANALYST JOB AT THE CIA?

So how does one get an analyst job at the CIA? Mine is not the most glamorous story. But for me, it all started with the online application. As far as I know, everybody who wants a job at CIA has to apply using the online application at CIA.gov.

CIA jobs are highly competitive. I remember a CIA Director saying that Harvard has a much higher acceptance rate than the CIA.

I put a lot of time and effort into my application and each of the application questions. I talked about how my experience working with the Canadian government would help me better understand what foreign leaders might be thinking and how they might act. I explained how I'm a man of action and "loathe irrelevant analysis." (my interviewer, after I was hired and I began working at the CIA, told me that that quote from my application really resonated with him).

I think my good, well thought out answers helped my application a lot. GPA seems to matter a lot, too.

My language skills were nothing special; I spoke Spanish at a basic level. I didn't have any special knowledge of or experience in any foreign countries outside of Canada, Mexico, and the UK, which aren't exactly CIA targets; I had actually studied American politics.

But I could think critically and write coherently. And I showed an understanding of what the CIA did (all learned from books and internet research) and I had a passion for the mission. That seemed to do the trick.

> "My #1 recommendation to anybody applying at CIA is to find somebody who works at the CIA and get them to flag your application."

My chat with Peter C. at the career fair also was important. CIA gets well over 50,000 applications per year, so it's easy for your application to get lost in the internet/government void. My #1 recommendation to anybody applying at CIA is to find somebody who works at the CIA and get them to flag your application. Outside of having some obscure, vital skill or speaking a critical language, this is the only way to have your application looked at closely. If you don't know anybody at the Agency, find a career fair or an event and talk to them. Ask them to put a referral for you into the system. That's what I did. It's truly that important.

Fortunately, the Agency was interested in my

application. They notified me of their interest and then sent me an online test to take. This was a scenario about a hypothetical country called Freelandia. I was presented with background information on Freelandia and then given new intelligence that had been "collected". Using that information, I was to analyze the situation and write my analysis to the President of Freelandia.

It was a good test, and it very closely matched the actual work that analysts do. To prepare, I researched the actual words that CIA analysts use in their papers, and then I mimicked that language on the test. I also researched the process that CIA analysts use to make their judgments, and applied that process. To say I was well-prepared would be an understatement.

Apparently I scored well on the test, because I was then invited to an interview. The interview was what CIA calls a "blitz". Around 100 people were invited and the blitz began with a presentation to all of us on the CIA and the rest of the application process. The next day, each of us interviewed one-on-one with the particular CIA offices that were interested in us. Interestingly, I had three offices that were interested in me. So, I interviewed with all three!

At least one of the offices decided to give me a Conditional Offer of Employment (COE). As amazing as it was to get to this point, unfortunately the COE doesn't mean a whole lot. It says that IF I get through the security clearance process and IF the job is still open when I pass the security clearance process, then I will be given a job. That's a lot of IFs!

The COE does include a salary amount, but that's about all it offers. If I didn't get approved for a Top Secret clearance, I didn't get the job. If the Agency gave 4 COEs for one analyst position, and one of the other 3 applicants completed the process before me, then I wouldn't get the job.

But it's still a good situation to be in. At this point, there was a decent chance that I'd be working at Langley within a year or two.

Why do I say "a year or two"? Because after the COE is the security clearance process, which can take an extremely long time and is highly variable depending on the individual's circumstances. Read on to learn more about the security clearance process.

The CIA actually has a job portal that, aside from the positions, looks like any other human resources portal.

6: The security clearance investigation

Edward Snowden, Robert Hanssen, Aldrich Ames. What do these names have in common?

These are just a few of the most notable people who held US security clearances and then (allegedly) leaked classified information, creating major damage to the United States.

Because CIA analysts have access to so much information that is vital to the country, it's important to make sure that the people who have access to that information are trustworthy.

This is why we have the security clearance process. The goal is to prevent hiring someone like Snowden, Hanssen, or Ames—to prevent such people from getting access to classified information.

And it's a long, intense process.

Like many government processes, it started with me filling out a long set of forms. The security clearance form is called the SF-86, and it required that I list everywhere I've lived, someone who knew me at that address, where I've traveled, where I've worked, and things like that.

This list helps get the lead investigator started in finding any potential skeletons in my closet.

> "The goal is to find any vulnerabilities that foreign intelligence services, or others, could exploit."

The goal is to find if I have any vulnerabilities that foreign intelligence services, or others, could exploit. If I'm someone who blows all my money and goes into debt, that's a problem because one day I might lose all my money and consider selling secrets to another country to pay my debts. If I'm someone who is married and cheats on my wife, a foreign intelligence service might learn about this and threaten to tell my wife if I don't give them classified information. If I'm someone who does a lot of drugs…you get the idea.

After filling out my form and then a long wait, the lead investigator gave me a call to let me know the background investigation was starting, and we had an in-person meeting. I say lead investigator because there was actually a team of investigators looking into me. The lead investigator was in Michigan, where I grew up and where most of my contacts were. There were other investigators, however, assigned to look into my contacts and activities in other places.

You might think that warning me that the investigation is starting is a bad idea. But don't worry, this didn't give me any ability to go tell my people to say only good things. The investigators know I'm not going to list anyone who's going to talk bad about me. These people are pros. One technique they use: each investigator goes to the places I have lived and talks with the neighbors. The goal is to find people who will speak frankly about me.

This process lasted months. And it was very cryptic. I had a contact I could call whenever I had questions. But, being the CIA, I only knew this person's first name and last initial. Jenny C. rarely had specific updates to provide me into this very secretive process. Each time I called, I received the same update. Everything was moving, and I'd hear from someone when the next stage was ready.

CIA isn't exactly known for its customer service.

*The security clearance process is extensive
because the US Government does not want just anybody
looking behind this Top Secret cover sheet.*

7: MEDICAL EXAMINATION & THE DREADED POLYGRAPH

After the background investigation and another lengthy wait, I was flown to Washington DC. My blood was drawn—I assume they were looking for health defects and perhaps more importantly, sexually transmitted diseases—and I was given a long psychology test. No, I don't like to play with fire. No, I don't hear voices in my head. No, I'm not crazy. (Ok, maybe a little crazy.) This test was followed by an interview with a psychologist.

Then, I was given the infamous polygraph. The polygraph is scary mostly because you HAVE to pass. This is not like a court of law, where you only have to worry about failing the polygraph. In court, an inconclusive polygraph can't put you in jail. But when you're applying for the CIA, if the polygraph comes up inconclusive, then you don't get a security clearance and you don't get the job. You have to actively pass the polygraph. So, when you're taking your poly, even if you know you have a clean background and are not lying, you fear that the machine will malfunction, that you'll breath the wrong way, that the polygrapher will have a bad day and make a mistake, or that your nervousness will make the results inconclusive. And then you'll be sent home looking for another job. Not a good feeling!

I've been sworn not to describe the details of my polygraph experience, so I can't tell you much. But I can say that the polygraph experience is not quite what is presented in the movies. There were surprisingly few questions. Maybe 10 questions. And I was told what the questions would be, in advance. There were no "gotcha" questions designed to catch me off guard. In fact, before the test, the polygrapher and I spent a good 30 minutes talking through the questions and clarifying them, so there would be no question about what they meant or what was intended.

> "My polygraph lasted nearly 6 hours spread over 2 days."

Those 10 questions, however, lasted nearly 6 hours spread over 2 days. It was a very intense, stressful process.

After the poly, it was time to "hurry up and wait," again. For months.

At this point, all of the information from each of these stages was combined into a file about me, which was given to an adjudicator to evaluate. There are no hard and fast rules on what will get you a clearance and what will make you ineligible, so no one can tell you if you're likely to get the clearance or not. It's all up to a mysterious adjudicator. And if the process takes too long, someone else might get in before you and take the job.

Fortunately, I ultimately was granted the Top Secret clearance, and I was formally offered the job of CIA analyst.

The entire security clearance process lasted more than a year.

A somewhat realistic depiction of the polygraph.
(Image courtesy of standret)

8: What's the first thing to do after receiving a security clearance? Get a raise!

I doubt many people do this—it's a little crazy to call up the mysterious, scary people at Langley who have cryptic names like "John P." or "Karen L.", and ask for more money. But that's exactly what I did when I was granted my security clearance.

My thinking, the security clearance process was long and it had been more than a year since I was given my Conditional Offer of Employment. In that time, I had gained more work experience, and perhaps most importantly, I now was more valuable because I had been approved for a security clearance!

Karen L. said she would take my request to the unknown people who make such decisions, who in retrospect most likely were the people in the specific office I would be working for. A few days later, I was told that I was approved for something like $3,000 per year more than I was initially offered.

Before I even started the job, I earned my first raise!

CHAPTER 3

CIA ANALYST? WHAT DOES THAT
MEAN...REALLY?

Many of us don't really know what a CIA analyst is. It can be hard to imagine what it is like to be a CIA analyst, day-to-day. What do analysts even do?

This chapter takes you behind the scenes and gives insight into the realities of being a CIA analyst.

Here are some highlights you'll find in this chapter.

9: What is an Intelligence analyst?

10. How do analysts compare to "spies"?

11. Hey new guy, go brief the Ambassador

12. Writing for the President of the United States

13. Protecting the Olympics

14. Do you have to be really smart to work at CIA?

15. Do CIA analysts have much passion?

16. Recognition is rare, but you can win awards

9: What is an Intelligence Analyst?

Jack Ryan was a CIA Intelligence analyst. But what does an analyst actually do?

Most analysts begin their day by firing up their computers, checking their e-mails, and then reading through the new intelligence cables. These cables are the key to analysts' work.

You've probably seen plenty of CIA spy movies, but those movies don't show what the CIA really does, for the most part. The CIA is in the business of information. The CIA "spies" are actually called case officers or operations officers. Their job is to recruit real spies—foreigners who provide information to the United States about their country. The spy gives information to the CIA case officer, who then writes the information into a cable that is sent to Langley. The cables usually include specific information on an event or person.

For example, a cable might have described where the Soviets were hiding their missiles. Or perhaps General Secretary Khrushchev's plans and intentions in Cuba.

That's where the analyst comes in. The analyst connects US policymakers with the intelligence. Our #1 customer is the President of the United States and his executive agencies—especially the National Security Council, the Department of Defense, and the State Department. We also often write for Congress. I've had my papers read by everybody from working-level analysts to Ambassadors to the President.

> "I've had my papers read by everybody from working-level analysts to Ambassadors to the President."

While case officers are good at coaxing information from spies and ensuring everybody's safety during secret meetings, analysts are the substantive experts. Analysts read many cables containing information from many spies over time, and then put the information into context and search for patterns and trends.

Here is an example. Keep in mind that this is an old example from the Soviet days to keep this book unclassified. If I used a more current example, this section might be covered with black boxes!

An analyst might receive a cable from a reliable source saying that Khrushchev wants to move SS-21 missiles into Cuba to attack Washington. Emergency?! Call up the President and warn him? Absolutely not. The Soviet missile analyst knows the range of an SS-

21 and realizes that such a missile could never reach Washington. Many people would overreact to the news, but that wouldn't be helpful to policymakers. The expert CIA analyst puts the information into perspective.

The next week, the analyst gets a cable from a questionable source saying that Khrushchev wants to move R-12 missiles into Cuba to attack Washington. The analyst knows that the R-12 could plausibly strike Washington from Cuba. Time to sound the alarms? It's not entirely clear. Could the source be lying? Could the Soviets intentionally be feeding us bad information through the source? Could the source think he's telling the truth but be mistaken? Even if the source is correct, how does the analyst know whether Khrushchev will follow through on his intentions or change his mind? Analysts have to make judgments about complex situations based on limited information that is often vague and contradictory.

Two weeks later, the analyst might get a report from imagery analysts indicating that something that looks like a disguised missile was being moved in Cuba. (Yes, analysts get to see the actual imagery photos, but it's hard for the untrained eye to make any sense of them. We often rely on the imagery analyst's report.)

Now is it time to warn the President? It just might be. Perhaps the analyst will spend the day writing a paper for the President's Daily Brief (PDB) the next morning.

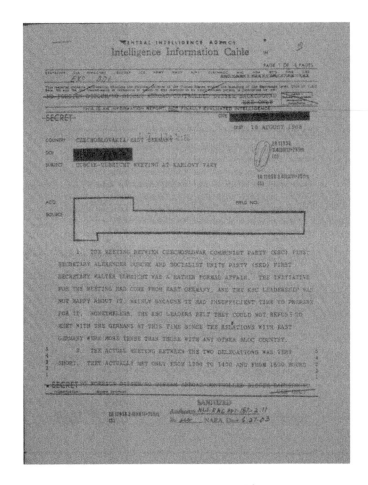

An example of a CIA cable.
(Photo courtesy of the University of Texas Libraries)

10. How do analysts compare to "spies"?

When you walk into a CIA office party, it's very clear who are the analysts and who are the "spies".

> "Analysts are likely to be sitting alone or
> sitting with a small group of other analysts."

The analysts are likely to be sitting alone or sitting with a small group of other analysts. The "spies" will be standing up and interacting with anyone and everyone. Analysts are typically the classic Myers-Briggs INTJ. Introverted. Detail-oriented. Thinkers, who rely heavily on logic and not so much on intuition. And they are planners who are typically very organized. And this personality fits their job. Analysts spend most of their day reading through reports and collating that information into a mental model to make judgments about the future.

CIA "spies" are the opposite. Highly extroverted. Intuitive. More in touch with their and others' feelings. A little more "go-with-the-flow" and able to adapt to situations. This personality also fits their job. A CIA "spy" needs to talk with everyone in the room to determine who has access to the information needed, and quickly befriend that person to initiate a relationship to obtain that information.

Now, these personality traits aren't universal, of course. But it was common enough that you could generally pick out who is whom at any CIA event. It was stark.

Both tended to be very smart, though, and very passionate about foreign current events and culture. CIA "spies" are not as smooth or James Bond-like as you might picture, or as portrayed in movies. Even CIA "spies" lean heavily toward the geeky side of the spectrum.

I actually found my personality right in the middle of the two sides. I got along very well with the "spies", and found myself befriending as many Case Officers as analysts. But I'm a Myers-Briggs ENTJ, and do not fit the classic analyst personality.

Analysts are likely to be sitting alone or with a small group of other analysts. (Photo by Andrea Piacquadio)

11. HEY NEW GUY, GO BRIEF THE AMBASSADOR

"Scott, you'll be briefing the Ambassador to ▮▮▮▮▮ next week."

(Author's Note and Apology: Bizarrely, the CIA insisted on redacting the name of the country.)

"Huh? I have about 2 weeks of experience and the Ambassador has been working on ▮▮▮▮▮ for 20 years."

"Don't worry about it. You'll do great."

The CIA does not handle analysts with kid gloves, and they did not hesitate to throw me into the deep end of the pool.

The Ambassador to ▮▮▮▮▮ is an especially intimidating position to brief. This is a Central Asian country that is not exactly a lovely place to visit or a desirable place to be posted. The Ambassador to somewhere nice like the United Kingdom...no problem. That's a coveted post that usually goes to a major campaign donor who knows very little about that country or foreign policy, in general.

President Trump's Ambassador to the UK, Woody Johnson, for example, was an heir to the Johnson and Johnson pharmaceutical fortune, ran a private investment firm, and bought the New York Jets football team. But he was a Republican National Committee Vice Chairman who was responsible for raising $1 billion to the Trump election campaigns and who personally donated $1.5 million. Nothing against Mr. Johnson, but I could have briefed most Ambassadors to the UK when I was in high school.

> "Not even the Ambassador to ██████
> wants to be the Ambassador to ███████."

But who wants to be Ambassador to ██████ ? Nobody. Not even the Ambassador to ██████ wants to be the Ambassador to ██████. And that's only a slight exaggeration. So, the post will usually be filled by a 20-year State Department veteran diplomat who has spent their entire career studying . They probably have developed a Stockholm-syndrome-esque love for ██████.

I didn't have much knowledge to share with the Ambassador, but I was able to provide the latest news and enjoyed my time speaking with him.

The Caucasus and Central Asia

Neither I nor the Ambassador to ▇▇▇▇▇ will be offended if you can't pick out ▇▇▇▇▇ on a blank map.

12. WRITING FOR THE PRESIDENT OF THE UNITED STATES

Writing for the President of the United States is typically the main goal for CIA analysts, and it's an awesome experience. Articles for the President go into the Presidential Daily Brief (PDB). The PDB is the gold-standard for intelligence analysts and is nearly always on an analyst's mind.

The President is the number one customer, and whenever you have the chance to write for the President, you do it.

The PDB process is intense. First, you have to find a topic that's worthy of the President's time. The bar is high. The President doesn't need to know about insignificant events. Does the topic significantly affect the United States? And, can the President do anything about it? Presidents don't like to be presented problems without solutions!

I wrote many papers for both George W. Bush and Barack Obama. This is because I tended to work on "hot topics" like South Asia and Latin America.

(Author note: My apologies, the CIA insisted I not name the actual countries.)

People who worked on quieter accounts—a European analyst, perhaps—may never write a PDB. Or, they might write one only every year or two.

Once you find the topic, you have to research it and write your paper. Then, you have to send it to the entire Intelligence Community that works on your topic—think FBI, Department of Defense, Department of Homeland Security, State Department, and others—for coordination. Often coordination can be a mess. A CIA analyst might write a paper suggesting a Department of Defense program is not going well, which DoD will be resistant to because…it's their program! They may genuinely think their program is going better than it really is, or they may actively try to suppress bad information even when they know their program is struggling, since their job, reputation, and funding may depend on it. Or, we might be wrong and just be too hard on them. Regardless, coordination can be very contentious and difficult.

Once you have consensus, or have decided to push ahead without consensus and allow another agency to attach a dissent to your paper, you then have to go through the review process. For me, first my manager would edit the paper. Then, the Deputy Group chief would edit. Then, the Group Chief. Then, the Deputy

Director. Then, the Director. Then, the Director of Intelligence would edit. Think you're done? No way, José! Next, is the PDB Editor, and then the Senior PDB Editor. All in all, it's somewhere around 10 editors.

In such a process, every period, every space, and every word is scrutinized. There will be debates over "probably" versus "likely". There will be zero ambiguity in the paper, by the end. CIA analysts learn to anticipate these edits, and ultimately become very precise writers.

Often this process will last late into the night. You might put in a 13-hour day and get home at 10 PM.

And then, the next morning, you get up at oh-dark-thirty (nobody in the Agency says zero-dark-thirty, despite the movie with that name) to meet with the PDB Briefer and the briefers for the other Cabinet members, like the Secretary of State, Secretary of Defense, and others. These people will read the article and ask you questions that they think the President or Cabinet member will ask them.

Then, they brief the paper to the person.

Around noon, we analysts attend an out-brief meeting to hear how things went. The scrutiny presented in these meetings is almost comical. The briefer might note that the President chuckled at a particular point of the paper, or that the Secretary of State paused and thought about something at this other point of the paper. And sometimes, after putting in all that work, the only feedback you would receive is "Read with interest."

The best feedback I ever received was that the President decided to schedule an Oval Office meeting devoted to discussing the ideas I highlighted in my PDB article. You can't ask for much more impact than that!

Here's a short example of what a PDB might look like. The PDB usually would include another paragraph or two, which I have left out for the sake of brevity. One might outline why Khrushchev might be moving the missiles or what he hopes to achieve. Another could lay out options or ideas for the President to address the situation.

Khrushchev Potentially Moving Long-Range Missiles to Cuba

Analysis of imagery indicates that missiles are being moved in Cuba. We lack reporting to determine the specific type of missiles being moved, but reporting suggests that the missiles could include Soviet long-range ballistic missiles intended to strike Washington, according to reporting.

- Analysis indicates that probable missiles were transported, most likely by ship, to Cuba.

- General Secretary Khrushchev intends to move R-12 missiles into Cuba to attack Washington.

Bin Ladin Determined To Strike in US

Clandestine, foreign government, and media reports indicate Bin Ladin since 1997 has wanted to conduct terrorist attacks in the US. Bin Ladin implied in US television interviews in 1997 and 1998 that his followers would follow the example of World Trade Center bomber Ramzi Yousel and "bring the fighting to America."

After US missile strikes on his base in Afghanistan in 1998, Bin Ladin told followers he wanted to retaliate in Washington, according to a ▒▒▒▒▒▒▒▒▒▒ service.

An Egyptian Islamic Jihad (EIJ) operative told an ▒▒▒▒▒ service at the same time that Bin Ladin was planning to exploit the operative's access to the US to mount a terrorist strike.

The millennium plotting in Canada in 1999 may have been part of Bin Ladin's first serious attempt to implement a terrorist strike in the US. Convicted plotter Ahmed Ressam has told the FBI that he conceived the idea to attack Los Angeles International Airport himself, but that Bin Ladin lieutenant Abu Zubaydah encouraged him and helped facilitate the operation. Ressam also said that in 1998 Abu Zubaydah was planning his own US attack.

Ressam says Bin Ladin was aware of the Los Angeles operation.

Although Bin Ladin has not succeeded, his attacks against the US Embassies in Kenya and Tanzania in 1998 demonstrate that he prepares operations years in advance and is not deterred by setbacks. Bin Ladin associates surveilled our Embassies in Nairobi and Dar es Salaam as early as 1993, and some members of the Nairobi cell planning the bombings were arrested and deported in 1997.

Al-Qa'ida members—including some who are US citizens—have resided in or traveled to the US for years, and the group apparently maintains a support structure that could aid attacks. Two al-Qa'ida members found guilty in the conspiracy to bomb our Embassies in East Africa were US citizens, and a senior EIJ member lived in California in the mid-1990s.

A clandestine source said in 1998 that a Bin Ladin cell in New York was recruiting Muslim-American youth for attacks.

We have not been able to corroborate some of the more sensational threat reporting, such as that from a ▒▒▒▒▒▒▒▒▒▒ service in 1998 saying that Bin Ladin wanted to hijack a US aircraft to gain the release of "Blind Shaykh" 'Umar 'Abd al-Rahman and other US-held extremists.

continued

For the President Only
6 August 2001

Here is the actual PDB article about Bin Laden's plans to attack the United States from August 2001, which has been declassified.

13. Protecting the Olympics

At one point of my analyst career, I was part of the team devoted to protecting the 2010 Olympics Winter Games in Vancouver. The team had 24/7 coverage, which meant I worked every day during the Olympics. My shift was in the afternoon, so I worked something like 3 pm to midnight.

I'll be honest, I applied largely because I wanted to spend a month in Vancouver. But this was another great experience that exemplifies what it's like to be a CIA analyst. It was a competitive process, but ultimately I was chosen to be part of the team. However, I was assigned to Washington DC.

> "Most of the time I was getting paid to watch the Jamaican bobsled team and ice dancing."

In truth, there was not a ton of intelligence regarding the Olympics. That means, most of the time I was getting paid to watch the Jamaican bobsled team and ice dancing.

However, on occasion there was intelligence to analyze and it was a thing of beauty to watch the efficiency of an inter-agency team, in which I represented CIA and worked closely with NSA, FBI, DIA, DHS, and many others.

In one case, I worked in coordination with representatives from other agencies to corroborate information and get a suspected terrorist on the Do No Fly List. Perhaps we prevented an attack on the games!

14. Do you have to be really smart to work at the CIA?

Honestly, yes. Everyone at the CIA is pretty smart and aggressively so. If anyone is less intelligent, they will be marginalized and generally won't be respected or accepted. It isn't necessarily right, but it's a sad reality.

> "If anyone is less intelligent, they will be marginalized."

I felt the impostor syndrome in my early days at The Agency, largely because everyone there is so articulate and smart, and they do not hesitate to show how smart they are. I've never met more Yale graduates in my life. And this is not the type of environment where people will take it easy on you or are careful about feelings. If you're wrong, you will be told so with no holds barred, perhaps even rudely.

I'm a smart guy, myself. I've always scored in the top 1% on aptitude tests and am a member of the Mensa High IQ Society based on my score on IQ tests. But even I felt intimidated at CIA.

The feeling faded, and I started to see that I did belong. But there's no question, being smart is a major advantage and is almost a necessity to work at the CIA.

Everyone at the CIA is smart and most go out of their way to show how smart they are. (Photo by Rene Asmussen)

15. DO CIA ANALYSTS HAVE MUCH PASSION?

Oh my, yes. CIA analysts have so much passion. More passion than you could ever imagine.

> "CIA Analysts regularly get into arguments about the topics they cover."

An example, CIA analysts will regularly get into arguments about the topics they cover. I'm not talking about an occasional disagreement that bubbles slightly out of control. I'm talking about regular, heated arguments.

This was the norm of the job. This is not a job where people punch a time-clock and go home. Nor is it a job for the faint of heart or people who prefer to avoid confrontation.

When we wrote for the President of the United States, the stakes became even higher. This was our top product and our #1 focus.

For PDBs, analysts would legitimately argue over "probably" versus "most likely". The arguments could become very specific and very passionate.

I remember one occasion where a disagreement became so heated, another analyst went too far and was quite mean to me. I didn't think too much of it; because it happened somewhat frequently.

But the next day, she apologized and bought me coffee to say she was sorry. It's a good example that analysts get very caught up in the topics they cover and can become very heated and passionate. But upon reflection, they typically realize when they have gone too far.

Arguing is the norm among CIA analysts.
(Photo by Antoni Shkraba)

16. RECOGNITION IS RARE, BUT YOU CAN WIN AWARDS IF YOU PERFORM EXCEPTIONALLY

CIA analysts mostly work in the shadows. When you write a paper, for example, your name is not even attached to the paper. It's not your paper, it's the CIA's paper.

This is not a job that receives public recognition. That's just the nature of the job.

However, CIA analysts can win awards, on occasion.

I'm not the most showy guy, but I like winning an award as much as the next person. I've won many awards in my tenure with the CIA, including multiple Exceptional Performance Awards.

The most prestigious award I received, however, was the National Intelligence Award. I won this award for my work on a National Intelligence Estimate on ███████████████████████████████████.

(Author's Note: My apologies, the CIA insisted that I redact the actual topic for which I won the award.)

At the awards ceremony, I was presented the award, along with all of the other award winners. It was a nice ceremony and a nice award.

My biggest surprise: I won the award the same year that terrorists set off a bomb at the Boston Marathon. That was one of the biggest terrorist attacks since 9/11. An FBI team responded to this Boston Marathon attack, extremely admirably I must say, and caught the perpetrators. This team received the same National Intelligence Award that I received. But that entire FBI team shared the same award that I received individually. I was shocked and honored.

CHAPTER 4

LIFE OUTSIDE THE OFFICE FOR A CIA
ANALYST

The previous chapter, describes what the life of a CIA
analyst is like while in the office.

However, CIA life is not a 9 to 5 affair. It affects your
entire life. This chapter focuses more on what life is
like outside the office for CIA analysts.

Here are some highlights you'll find in this chapter.

17: How much do CIA analysts earn?

18: Where do CIA analysts live?

**19: The question every CIA analyst dreads:
"Where do you work?"**

**20. Does the CIA care what former analysts write
& say in the media?**

21: You're at a bar and see a CIA friend who is undercover. What do you do?

17: HOW MUCH DO CIA ANALYSTS EARN?

Government employees aren't generally known to be highly paid. CIA analysts, however, are highly skilled and usually are paid pretty well.

The CIA uses the US Government's General Schedule (GS). I started in 2007 as a GS-9, making around $58,000 per year ($74,000 in 2021 dollars) right out of graduate school with no experience.

I earned 4 promotions in my 7 years. Each promotion adds one grade to your GS level. I left The Agency in 2015 as a GS-13 making $97,000 ($108,000 in 2021 dollars).

SALARY TABLE 2022-DCB
INCORPORATING THE 2.2% GENERAL SCHEDULE INCREASE AND A LOCALITY PAYMENT OF 31.53%
FOR THE LOCALITY PAY AREA OF WASHINGTON-BALTIMORE-ARLINGTON, DC-MD-VA-WV-PA
TOTAL INCREASE: 3.02%
EFFECTIVE JANUARY 2022

Annual Rates by Grade and Step

Grade	Step 1	Step 2	Step 3	Step 4	Step 5	Step 6	Step 7	Step 8	Step 9	Step 10
1	$ 26,532	$ 27,423	$ 28,304	$ 29,183	$ 30,064	$ 30,579	$ 31,453	$ 32,331	$ 32,367	$ 33,190
2	29,834	30,544	31,532	32,367	32,733	33,695	34,658	35,621	36,584	37,547
3	32,552	33,637	34,723	35,808	36,893	37,978	39,063	40,148	41,233	42,318
4	36,542	37,760	38,978	40,196	41,414	42,632	43,849	45,067	46,285	47,503
5	40,883	42,246	43,609	44,971	46,334	47,697	49,059	50,422	51,785	53,147
6	45,574	47,093	48,612	50,131	51,651	53,170	54,689	56,208	57,727	59,246
7	50,643	52,331	54,018	55,706	57,393	59,081	60,768	62,456	64,143	65,831
8	56,086	57,955	59,824	61,693	63,562	65,431	67,300	69,169	71,038	72,907
9	61,947	64,012	66,077	68,142	70,207	72,272	74,337	76,402	78,467	80,532
10	68,217	70,491	72,765	75,039	77,313	79,587	81,862	84,136	86,410	88,684
11	74,950	77,447	79,945	82,443	84,941	87,439	89,936	92,434	94,932	97,430
12	89,834	92,829	95,824	98,818	101,813	104,808	107,803	110,798	113,793	116,788
13	106,823	110,384	113,944	117,505	121,065	124,626	128,187	131,747	135,308	138,868
14	126,233	130,441	134,649	138,856	143,064	147,272	151,479	155,687	159,894	164,102
15	148,484	153,434	158,383	163,333	168,282	173,232	176,300 *	176,300 *	176,300 *	176,300 *

Federal payscale. (Courtesy of the US Office of Personnel Management)

18: WHERE DO CIA ANALYSTS LIVE?

Because they earn decent salaries, most CIA analysts live pretty well and can afford nice apartments. I had a one bedroom apartment in the Rosslyn neighborhood in Arlington, Virginia, which is walking distance to the famous Georgetown area.

This put me close to Washington DC and the most vibrant areas, while also being just a short drive up the George Washington Parkway to CIA Headquarters at Langley. With no traffic (an oxymoron in Washington DC), the 7-mile drive took about 15 minutes.

My apartment had an amazing view of the Lincoln Monument, the Washington Monument, and the Capitol Building, as you can see in this photo.

CIA analysts typically live throughout the entire Washington DC area. Many analysts live in Arlington, Virginia because it was "cool" while still being close to Langley. Others prefer areas to live in Washington DC, like Adams Morgan.

The Real Jack Ryan at his apartment in the Rosslyn neighborhood in Arlington, Virginia.

19: THE QUESTION EVERY CIA ANALYST DREADS: "WHERE DO YOU WORK?"

If you work at CIA, eventually you'll dread the common question of small talk, "Where do you work?"

Covert employees like "spies" are under cover and cannot acknowledge their affiliation with CIA. It's actually simpler for them, because their cover provides them with a story to answer this question.

Most analysts, though, are overt, which means they openly work for CIA. We even received tax forms at the end of the year that say "CIA" on them! Overt employees technically can admit they work for CIA. But they typically won't want to publicize their CIA affiliation. CIA analysts have great access to classified information and foreign intelligence services might target a known CIA analyst to spy against the United States.

However, overt employees aren't given a cover story. So when asked, "Where do you work?", different people handle the question differently. Some are very secretive–one overt employee told me she had not told her parents where she worked–while others will respond truthfully. Both, however, dread the question.

We were given widely varying advice on what to say to people. My favorite was to say, "I work for the government." Umm, ok. Because nobody in Washington DC will know what that means. This was not the best advice, because the obvious next question would be, "Which agency?" Then you're back at square one.

"Just be really boring, so they stop asking."

The other recommended approach was, "Just describe what you do and make it sound really boring, so they stop asking."

CIA analysts weren't exactly known to be social butterflies, and this fit the mold. Just be really boring.

"Just describe what you do and make it sound really boring, so they stop asking." (Photo by Andrea Piacquadio)

20. Does the CIA care what former analysts write & say in the media?

Yes. Very much, yes.

Everything I write that has anything to do with the CIA, intelligence, or a topic I covered while at the CIA needs to be approved by the CIA's Publications Review Board. This even includes résumés and CVs.

This is true for all CIA analysts, current and past.

Not to say this is unreasonable. Usually, the review board just looks for anything that shouldn't be published, doesn't find much that is objectionable (most of us aren't trying to publish anything classified or sensitive), and then approves the publication.

But the CIA very much cares about what we all write in the media. And we've agreed to be monitored on this topic for the rest of our lives.

> "The CIA reviewed this book, and made edits and deletions."

Even this book was reviewed by the CIA's

Publications Review Board. And they also insisted that some edits and deletions were made.

Photo created by Dale-E Artificial Intelligence.

21: You're at a bar and see a CIA friend who is undercover. What do you do?

This isn't something many people think about. Analysts are overt, which means they openly work for CIA, but they work closely with many people, including "spies" who were undercover. When you work closely with people, you can often get to know each other well and become friends.

But what happens when you, an overt analyst, go to your favorite bar or restaurant and see your friend, who is undercover?

Normally, if you see a friend when you're out, you are excited to say hello to them. But nothing about CIA life is normal!

Because I was overt, many people knew I worked at CIA. If someone overt, like me, talked to someone undercover in public, that could blow their cover.

Maybe this undercover person tells people that they "work for another part of the government" or that they do something completely different. If I ran up and said hello to my undercover friend in public, it would raise the question, "Why is this person talking to a CIA officer?"

"Ignore him or her, to preserve their cover."

The general protocol, believe it or not, is that when an overt analyst like me sees an undercover friend in public, I am supposed to ignore him or her, to preserve their cover. If the person undercover talks to me, then it's fine. It's up to them, if they want to risk their cover. But that's their decision, not mine.

Can you imagine seeing a work friend when you're out, being excited to say hello, and having to act like you don't know them? Only in the world of The Real Jack Ryan!

Photo by Cotton Video and Graphics.

Chapter 5

Behind The Scenes: What's Langley Really Like?

It's hard to imagine, what is it really like at CIA Headquarters? Over 7 years, I probably spent around 15,000 hours there. In that time, Langley loses a bit of its mystique and becomes a real place. In this chapter, we'll get a feel for what the CIA really is like, without the mystique.

Here are some highlights you'll find in this chapter.

22. The real Langley

23. What do CIA analysts wear to work?

24. What is lunch like at CIA Headquarters?

25. Langley has a Family Day every year. Who wants to put Mom under the polygraph?

26. You do meet famous people at Langley

22. THE REAL LANGLEY

Langley, Virginia is where most intelligence analysis takes place. You might expect a hidden compound, but instead you'll find road signs directing you to the George Bush Center for Intelligence. The road signs even say "CIA" on them. Not the most secretive introduction.

You might expect a hidden compound, but instead you'll find road signs directing you to the CIA. (Photo by famartin)

But then you'll be greeted by guards with large rifles, which feels more like something you'd see in the movies. The feeling doesn't last long, however, because next you'll reach the parking lots.

A lot of people work at Langley, which makes parking spots difficult to find and usually far from the building. If you arrive at 8:30 A.M., expect a 10-minute walk to get into the building.

Walking through Langley the first time, I was struck by how similar the compound felt to a college campus. It was vibrant, full of people strolling about. Overall, you don't get the sense that you're in a building full of spooks. Everybody looks like normal people.

The courtyard is quite nice. It's full of trees and has a fountain and an odd sculpture called Kryptos to remind you where you are. Kryptos is a sculpture in code. Three-fourths of Kryptos has been cracked, but one section remains unsolved.

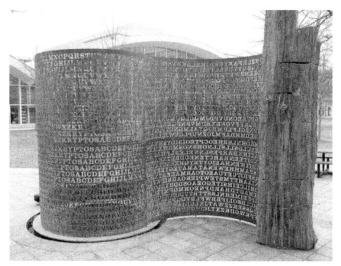

Kryptos, in the CIA courtyard. (Photo courtesy of CIA)

Don't like to take your work home with you? You're in luck. CIA won't let you.

Because almost all of our work involved classified information, it had to be done in a Sensitive Compartmented Information Facility (SCIF), which is essentially an entire office that is a safe or a vault. Work has to stay in the SCIF in Langley.

Usually it's nice to keep work and home separate. At home you never are burdened with the thought that you could be doing work. However, it can be a pain if you're at home but you need to know something on the classified computers. On Sunday, you might want to check your calendar for Monday, but you'd have to drive to Langley to do so.

23. What do CIA analysts wear to work?

My first time at CIA Headquarters, I expected a stuffy atmosphere and black suits. But this image was wrong. Nobody wore sunglasses to work, nor tuxedos. A surprising number of analysts often don't wear ties.

On Fridays, most people wear jeans, and even Hawaiian shirts. Of course, suits are required when interacting with people outside of the Agency, so there is an interesting mix of people who are dressed extremely well and those who look more casual.

Would you believe that the CIA has a formal dress code in its policies? It's a relic from the past, however, and was not well-known or enforced. The dress code has rules straight out of the 1950's, mostly offensive commentary surrounding what's appropriate for women to wear.

> "Dress pants, dress shirt with the top button unfastened, no tie."

There was an informal "analyst Uniform", particularly

for male analysts. Dress pants, dress shirt with the top button unfastened, no tie. Business casual at its finest, and the uniform was almost universal. analysts rarely wore ties and rarely wore suit jackets. We each kept a suit jacket and tie on hand, however, in case a briefing or important meeting came up unexpectedly.

Basically, the uniform was the most casual attire that could be transformed into a suit within 30 seconds. Like James Bond, we also could change our appearance in mere seconds.

Attire for female analysts was a little more varied. They might wear skirts, pants, dress shirts, or sweaters.

The CIA analyst uniform.
(Photo by LinkedIn)

24. WHAT IS LUNCH LIKE AT CIA HEADQUARTERS?

Most CIA analysts stay at headquarters for lunch. Some people go to restaurants on occasion, but the Langley compound is pretty isolated. It's almost impossible to eat lunch at a restaurant and make it back during your 30 minute lunch break. So you'd probably have to work late to make up for the lunch.

The café is large and is pretty nice. There's a traditional cafeteria with two or three entrée selections, soup choices, salad bar, sandwiches, and a grille. The food is usually pretty good, healthy, and there are many selections to choose from. However, portion sizes tend to be small and it's hard to find a good value.

There's also a fast food section, which at that time had Sbarros, Subway, Burger King, Chinese food, barbecue, Dunkin' Donuts, and Starbucks. You can get more food here for less money, but it's not the healthiest.

Most CIA analysts eat at their desks. They typically

don't want to take time away from their work. I was an exception. I found that the time away from the desk helped me think more creatively and clearly, and led me to think of analytic insights that I wouldn't have come up with, otherwise.

However, plenty of people eat in the café's large seating areas. When the weather is nice, you can also eat in a gorgeous courtyard, which was my favorite place to eat. It's not your typical courtyard, however. When you open the door, you'll see a sign reminding you not to bring classified material outside into the courtyard.

> "What this really means is that whenever I ate lunch, foreign spy satellites could see that I was eating Burger King and reading the Economist!"

The reason: foreign satellites can zoom in close enough to read any documents you bring to the courtyard, intended to read any classified material brought outside by mistake. What this really means is that whenever I ate lunch, foreign spy satellites could see that I was eating Burger King and reading the Economist!

The CIA courtyard.
(Photo courtesy of CIA)

25. Langley has a Family Day every year. Who wants to put Mom under the polygraph?

Once a year, CIA has a Family Day.

This is the day when your family is allowed to visit CIA Headquarters and CIA offices set up booths and organize events. As bizarre as it sounds, CIA Headquarters at Langley–generally portrayed as an amazing, almost mythical place—basically becomes a carnival for a day.

> "CIA Headquarters at Langley basically becomes a carnival for a day."

My family has met many CIA Directors at Family Day. General Mike Hayden, a big Pittsburgh Steelers fan, gave my Mom fantasy football advice regarding Ben Roethlisberger. Leon Panetta gave my Mom Italian restaurant recommendations in Detroit. Or perhaps Mom gave Mr. Panetta restaurant recommendations!

My Grandma, a prolific shopper, has scoured the CIA gift shop to find the most unique item of clothing.

Family Day is one of the most comical days, when comparing Langley to the movies. Why don't any of the movies show my Grandma in the gift shop?

One of my favorite "carnival rides" at Family Day is the lie detector test. Polygraphers are trained at administering lie detector tests and determining if a given terrorist is telling the truth or lying. At Family Day, however, the polygraphers focus their efforts on putting your parents onto the truth machine.

My Mom, according to the polygraph, was found to be truthful in that she is proud of me, but also truthful in that she does not own too many shoes...which I question!

A plaque from CIA's 36th Family Day.
(Photo by CIA posted on Twitter)

26. YOU DO MEET FAMOUS PEOPLE AT LANGLEY

Because it's the CIA, a fair amount of famous people come to visit.

I met Kenny Rogers and Kevin Bacon at CIA Headquarters. Many other famous people visited who I didn't bother to go meet. Or I couldn't because I actually had important work to do.

Have you ever played 6-degrees of Kevin Bacon, the game where you can link nearly any actor to Kevin Bacon within 6 degrees of separation only using movies in which both actors appear? Now you can play 7-Degrees of The Real Jack Ryan!

The real Jack Ryan with Kevin Bacon at CIA headquarters.

CHAPTER 6

THE FUN, INTERESTING & JUICY SECRETS OF THE CIA

You've all seen the movies. Is that what it's really like working at the CIA?

Of course not!

I'm often asked what it's really like working at CIA. What are the juicy details?

I of course am limited in what I can share, as much of the work is secretive and classified. But for this chapter, I've thought of everything fun, interesting, or juicy that I can share that is unclassified and that I could get approved for publication by the CIA.

Here are some highlights you'll find in this chapter:

27. If you had Top Secret access, what would you look up first?

28. Why are so many CIA officers having sex with a woman named FNU LNU?

29. Were you undercover?

30. How dumb were the bosses?

31. How do you dispose of classified information?

32. Do they haze new CIA employees?

33. Did you have CIA business cards?

34. What are CIA e-mails and messages like? Extremely formal and serious?

35. If your name is Scott, why are people calling you Rothy? (A.k.a what is a pseudo?)

36. What's the White House really like?

37. Why did you leave your cell phone in the car?

27. IF YOU HAD TOP SECRET ACCESS, WHAT WOULD YOU LOOK UP FIRST?

Imagine you had access to all of the CIA's Top Secret files. What would you look up first?

For me, the answer was easy. Aliens!

Without revealing anything secretive, I can tell you with confidence that alien conspiracy theories are not true. Aliens do not exist, as far as we know, and the CIA does not have any aliens or any information suggesting aliens have visited our planet.

> "Wow, I never would have guessed that person worked with CIA."

Another interesting topic is former CIA spies. There are definitely cases where certain people are, or throughout history were, CIA spies or assets that make you think, "Wow, I never would have guessed that person worked with CIA." This happens more than I would have guessed, and there are more people throughout world history that had some involvement in supporting the CIA than I would have guessed. I truly wish I could share some names with you.

It gives you a different perspective of world history, much of which is at most only partially accurate or is just part of the story.

28. Why are so many CIA officers having sex with a woman named FNU LNU?

For CIA officers stationed abroad, you can imagine that they might find themselves having "close contact" with plenty of foreign women. One-night-stands happen to be considered "close contact" with foreigners, and need to be reported to the CIA.

But with one night stands, you don't always know the other person's full name. In that case, a placeholder name would be used.

For instance, if you knew the woman's name was Francesca, but you didn't know her last name, you would report that you had "close contact" with Francesca LNU (Last Name Unknown).

Or if you knew someone's last name was Jones, but you didn't know her first name, you would use FNU Jones (First Name Unknown).

And people would pronounce these acronyms as if they were names. FNU LNU would be "Fah-new La-new".

> "Wow, this Fah-new La-new girl really gets around!"

There was a running joke in the CIA that somebody reviewing these "close contact" reports exclaimed, "Wow, this Fah-new La-new girl really gets around!"

It turns out there were many reports with the name FNU LNU (First Name Unknown Last Name Unknown) because it would be the name reported every time an officer slept with someone whose name they did not know at all!

It's worth noting that this phenomenon was not exclusive to men. Female officers had "close contact" with plenty of FNU LNUs, also.

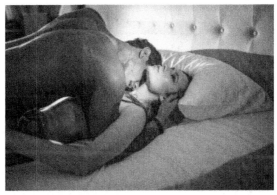

Be sure to report your close contact with First Name Unknown Last Name Unknown (FNU LNU)! (Photo by W R)

29. Were you undercover?

I was not undercover, usually…

At the Agency, most analysts are overt. This means they don't have a cover. They are known CIA officers.

We even received a W-2 each year saying Central Intelligence Agency on it!

I did go undercover, on occasion. It was not very deep cover, however. ████████████████████
(Author's note: The CIA redacted this portion that potentially revealed some details about cover)

Most spy types ███████████████ lived their cover every day of their lives. They often didn't even tell their husbands, wives, or family where they truly worked.

For those of us who were overt, it became a little awkward. You don't want to go around telling the world you work at CIA. You'd just be asking to become a target. You would never post on Facebook or LinkedIn that you were a CIA officer. But we didn't have any cover to help us accomplish this.

Cover is expensive for the government to maintain.

For this reason, many analysts created their own versions of a light cover, within the limits of the law, of course. Since we were overt, it was illegal for us to say we worked for an office, agency, or company that we didn't actually work for.

One example might be to say the name of your office instead of CIA. For instance, I could honestly say I worked for the more innocuous sounding Crime and Narcotics Center (which just happened to be part of the CIA.)

To be honest, I'm not sure if people did this for safety and security reasons or to feel important and cool. This was not something I did. Since I was overt, I was generally open and honest about where I worked.

I was in the minority, though. I guess that explains why I'm the one writing this book!

30. How dumb were the bosses?

It's easy to get lost in the CIA mystique, but the real day-to-day life at CIA is more like The Office than Jason Bourne.

My CIA co-worker/friend Rod and I would often say, "If only people knew what really goes on here."

The short answer is yes, I had plenty of stupid bosses.

One boss denied a useful trip because "It would be too fun."

On the flip side, we once proposed a trip to shoot AK-47's and presented it as "familiarization." Familiarization is when you spend time in a country you're going to be analyzing so that you are more familiar with the culture and the places you will be analyzing, so you can provide better-informed analysis. Two of our bosses actually approved the AK-47 training, but the third boss wisely denied it.

"Two of our bosses actually approved AK-47 training."

Brilliant analytic papers would get held up in review because a boss's boss just didn't understand it, or was not "comfortable" with the analytic message.

One manager told me, "I can't quite explain what's off with this paper, but it just isn't right."

The list goes on and on.

And don't get me wrong, I had many brilliant bosses. One was a Jeopardy champion, even.

But yes, the CIA is not above throwing a Michael Scott "The Office"-type boss your way, every now and then.

Photo by Andrea Piacquadio.

31. How do you dispose of classified information?

This is something people don't think about much, but what do you do with classified information when you're done with it? You can't just toss it in the trash!

It's not quite like the movies. You don't throw the document in your mouth and swallow it. Nor does classified information self-destruct after 5 seconds.

CIA analysts actually have "burn bags."

We would each have a bag at our desk and we would throw classified information into the bag. When the burn bag was full, we would have to walk it to a burn bag chute, which is like a big trash chute. The trash chute went to an incinerator where, as far as I know, where the burn bag was…burned. We also each had a normal trash bin at our desks, for unclassified trash. The burn bag is noticeably different from a standard trash bin, to ensure no classified information is mistakenly thrown into the trash.

A burn bag for the disposal of classified information.
(Photo courtesy of the US Department of Defense.)

32. Do they haze new CIA employees?

Definitely.

Each employee has a CIA ID number, which is used to identify that person. This number is used for many things, and CIA officers quickly memorize their ID number.

CIA veterans tell new employees that it's required that they yell out their ID number when throwing burn bags down the burn bag chutes.

None of the hazing is too crazy, but it's certainly funny to hear a newbie yelling their ID number unnecessarily when using a simple trash chute!

On a more serious level, there is latent hazing regarding something called "DI style". (The name has probably changed) DI is the Directorate of Intelligence, which is the analysis directorate.

This "DI style" of analysis and writing is arcane and mostly undefined. A veteran might say that something is not "DI style." But this was kind of a cop out, and was mostly just a way for a veteran to say they didn't like the work of a less-experienced analyst, without having to specifically say why. I had one manager reject a paper I had written saying, "I can't explain why it's not good, but I'll know a better paper when I see it."

Eventually, after years of this absurdity, you end up learning the ways to think and communicate that make veteran CIA analysts happy. And then they stop using this objection. But it takes a long time, and not all analysts master it.

This sort of hazing is more systemic and problematic, and should be addressed by CIA leadership.

Burn bag hazing...well, maybe we should let that one continue!

Trash chute drawing created by Artificial Intelligence Dall-E.

33. DID YOU HAVE CIA BUSINESS CARDS?

Believe it or not, I actually had CIA business cards.

I may have been the only CIA analyst who had them. Analysts are not under cover, so technically there is nothing wrong with having business cards. But analysts are generally not open about where they work. Business cards are not very CIA-esque.

But I saw the value in having business cards, mostly for networking with other agencies in the US Government. I would often attend US Government meetings to learn what they were working on, which in turn taught me what information they needed to better accomplish their goals.

I would then ensure that our spies were stealing this information so I could use the information in my reports, ultimately helping the government do its job better.

At these meetings, everyone would hand out business cards to each other, but the CIA officers never had business cards. So I decided I wanted business cards, too, so I could properly network like the others at the meetings.

> "I never would have guessed how difficult something like business cards would be, at the CIA!"

I never would have guessed how difficult something like business cards would be, at the CIA! At first, nobody wanted to approve me getting business cards. Managers just assumed we were CIA, and that business cards were not allowed because we were CIA.

But ultimately, I found an internal CIA regulation on business cards, which included all of the details and rules. With this regulation in hand, I was able to get approval for my business cards.

Why don't any of the CIA movies show the protagonist heroically wading through the bureaucracy to get business cards? The Real Jack Ryan can do this masterfully!

Jack P. Ryan
Deputy Director
Intelligence

Central Intelligence Agency
Washington, D.C. 20505

Tel. (703) 482-0623
Fax (703) 482-1739

34. What are CIA e-mails and messages like? Extremely formal and serious?

When envisioning the CIA, you might think e-mails would be very serious and formal. But you'd be wrong. Surprisingly, e-mails were extremely friendly. Almost to the point of being weird.

> "E-mails were extremely friendly. Almost to the point of being weird."

E-mails consistently would be written with a friendly introduction, "Hi Jack, how are you?" Then they would discuss the items of business.

But then the body of the e-mail would often be extremely critical. Finally, e-mails would often end with something friendly.

This was called the compliment sandwich, and is something that was taught to managers at CIA. However, I'd say it was more of a whiplash sandwich!

I found it very weird, almost over the top. And I honestly have no idea why this culture developed. When people sent me e-mails, they didn't actually care how my day was. But almost every e-mail at CIA was written this way.

Photo by Photo by Torsten Dettlaff.

35. IF YOUR NAME IS SCOTT, WHY ARE PEOPLE CALLING YOU ROTHY? (A.K.A WHAT IS A PSEUDO?)

At CIA, there is an internal instant messaging system that includes everybody in the CIA.

People who were undercover would have a pseudonym ██████████████.

And these people, even if you knew their real name, would end up being known in person by their pseudonym.

For instance, while my name is obviously Scott Schlimmer, if I were undercover I might be given the pseudo James P Rothingham ████.
(Author's note: My apologies, the CIA asked for a redaction, here)

And then my colleagues, in person, might refer to me as Roth or Rothy because of my pseudo.

It's amazing the impact a pseudo might have on you for your whole career. It was very impactful if you got a cool pseudo or a weird pseudo, early on.

I, however, as an overt officer, did not have a pseudonym. I showed up in the messaging system under my true name.

Photo by Heiner.

36. WHAT'S THE WHITE HOUSE REALLY LIKE?

You see it in all the movies and in the news, and it looks amazing. But what is the White House really like?

Honestly, I found the White House underwhelming. It was smaller than I expected, and not that impressive.

My first time going to the White House was unique. There are almost always protesters or advocates outside the White House. And they don't know who is important and who just a few months ago was unemployed, with me of course being the latter.

> "The protesters don't know who is important and who just a few months ago was unemployed, with me of course being the latter."

So these advocates approach everyone entering and plead their cause. It was bizarre to me, because I was just the new guy amazed to be visiting the White House for the first time on official business.

Inside the White House, everything is smaller than you would expect. The Situation Room was particularly small. There is a conference room in the Situation Room where they took a famous photo of President Obama during the raids on Osama Bin Laden. I briefed National Security Directors in this conference room, and it was just a small boring conference room!

One cool thing, The White House Mess (this means cafeteria) gave out White House M&Ms. These were great gifts for family and friends!

The Real Jack Ryan at the White House.

37. WHY DID YOU LEAVE YOUR CELL PHONE IN THE CAR?

Cell phones are not allowed in CIA Headquarters.

I never was the kind of person who was attached to his cell phone. I'd much prefer to turn the thing off and not be bothered.

I'm not sure if this was a result of working at the CIA or if I had this preference beforehand, which made me ok with CIA not allowing me to bring my cell phone to work.

But cell phones are strictly not allowed at CIA Headquarters. So, we became used to not having a cell phone for 8 or more hours per day.

> "We became used to not having a cell phone for 8 or more hours per day."

Loved ones, then, were used to the idea that they might not be able to get a hold of us. We had landlines at our desks, but CIA analysts are often away from their desks.

Every now and then, someone would slip up and bring their cell phone into the office. Usually it wasn't a huge deal. Cell phones didn't work in the building for the most part, anyways, because business is conducted inside Sensitive Compartmented Information Facilities (SCIFs), which are essentially entire offices that are large safes or vaults.

But if anyone made the mistake too many times and repeatedly brought their cell phone into Langley, then it would be treated as a security violation.

The cell phones of CIA analysts
spend a lot of time in the car's glove compartment.
(Drawing by Artificial Intelligence Dall-E)

Chapter 7

"You Can't Make This Sh*t Up!" (Stories That Could Only Happen to a CIA Analyst)

Reality is often more dramatic and funnier than the best Hollywood writers can imagine.

This chapter focuses on the more bizarre, dramatic, and humorous oddities of working at the CIA. You seriously can't make this sh*t up!

Here are some highlights you'll find in this chapter.

38. The time spies broke into my hotel room

39. The time I told Stevie Wonder about Tajikistan

40. The time CIA made me break up with my girlfriend

41. Diarrhea in the name of diplomacy

42. You know that guy you just offered cocaine to? He's with the CIA.

43. CIA analyst traveling for pleasure forgets to secure a visa?!

44. What job do you take after leaving the CIA?

38. THE TIME SPIES BROKE INTO MY HOTEL ROOM

I was in a former-Soviet country that has a very KGB-like intelligence service. Keep in mind, these "intelligence services" are like the CIA, but they are run by other countries.

I was only in the country for analytic exchanges, just meeting with US personnel to talk about the latest developments. But that country's intelligence service didn't know why I was there or what my goals were. In their minds, perhaps I was there to steal information. They can't tell the difference between a "spy" and someone like me, who is there for more innocuous reasons.

When I arrived, it was the end of winter, probably March or April, and my hotel room was very warm. Because it was hot, I called the front desk and asked if there was any way to make the temperature in my room cooler. They said no, because spring was afoot and the hotel's heat was still running and the air conditioning was not yet turned on. The entire building would switch over to air conditioning when winter was over and spring had officially begun. Very Soviet!

Ok, no big deal. Just a mild discomfort.

The next day, I went to the Embassy and had my meetings. When I returned in the evening, I saw all of my bags and things I had unpacked had been moved around. After a few seconds, I realized, "Wow, it's *really* hot in here." I checked the thermostat...and it was set at the highest setting. The heat had been turned on full blast!

> "I saw all of my bags and things I had
> unpacked had been moved around."

Apparently, the intelligence service listened to my phone call with the hotel staff complaining that the heat was too high or perhaps the hotel staff told the intelligence service about the conversation. The intelligence service must have broken into my room and moved around my bags and turned up the heat. Or the hotel gave them the keys.

Why?

It's hard to say exactly, but it's a bit of an intimidation tactic. A reminder: "We know you're here, and we're watching you."

This wasn't too bad, and it didn't particularly scare me.

But I have heard worse stories from other analysts. Intelligence services have gone into the hotel room of other CIA analysts when they were in the shower.

Can you imagine seeing someone's face in the reflection in the mirror while you're shaving or washing your face? This has happened.

Scary stuff!

A depiction of spies breaking into my hotel room drawn by Artificial Intelligence. (Dalle-E)

39. THE TIME I TOLD STEVIE WONDER ABOUT TAJIKISTAN

When I went to Tajikistan for meetings, I went to a restaurant and there was a man singing.

Tajikistan is a small country between Russia and Afghanistan. This means the people there speak a combination of Russian and Tajik Arabic. Almost no one there spoke English. So, you can imagine how shocked I was when I heard the singer sing a Stevie Wonder song in perfect English.

> "The singer just happened to memorize this one Stevie Wonder song."

I walked up to the singer and gave him a tip, and even more shockingly, he didn't understand a word I said. He didn't speak a word of English. The singer just happened to memorize this one Stevie Wonder song, presumably for that occasion to earn a tip when an American walked in.

Not long later, I was back in Washington and found myself at the Apple Store in Arlington Virginia, buying my first smartphone. I was a little behind the times, since cell phones aren't allowed into CIA headquarters.

I looked across the store, and who did I see? Stevie Wonder, of course! It turns out that Stevie has a close relationship with Apple because Apple does a lot of great work for the visually impaired.

I went over to speak with Stevie, and of course to tell him about my experience hearing his song across the world in Tajikistan, 6,500 miles away, sung by a man who didn't speak English.

I genuinely expected Stevie to say something amazing, and to set the perfect punchline to a great story of the most unlikely occurrences.

Instead, he said "Tajikistan…never heard of that place before."

Stevie :-(

The Real Jack Ryan with Stevie Wonder.

40. The time CIA made me break up with my girlfriend

As we drove by a foreign Embassy, I asked, "Hey, you're a US citizen, right?"

I knew she was born in another country, but she had lived in the United States for 20 years. She was as American as anyone else I had ever dated. It hadn't even crossed my mind to ask.

But she was not a US citizen.

Through friends—both trusted Americans, I should add—I was introduced to Marta. Marta was in her late 20s and was born in Ukraine, but had lived in the United States for most of her life. She didn't even have an accent. You wouldn't find her any different from anyone else, except for a few interesting stories about being a child in the Soviet Union.

I really liked Marta, and thought things could potentially progress into something long term.

During our 3rd date, we were driving by the Russian

Embassy, and I was almost just joking when I asked her if she was a citizen, figuring that someone who seemed so American and had lived in the United States for 20 years would of course be a US Citizen.

It turned out, Marta had never applied for US citizenship. And to the CIA, that made her a foreigner. And that meant I had to report her to the CIA to get approval to date her.

> "I had to report Marta to the CIA to get approval to date her."

I reported the "close contact" with a foreigner. Except this was very much not with FNU LNU!

The relationship was ultimately denied. I was also found to have committed a security violation, which was added to my record, for continuing to see Marta even after learning that she was not a US citizen. (But I did not continue to see her after the relationship was denied, of course.)

The whole thing was absurd and was extremely demotivating. The CIA wouldn't let me date a woman I really liked, and who had no indications of being anything other than an upstanding (albeit non-citizen) American.

For normal people, there would be no harm in dating Marta. But for a CIA analyst, this poses a serious complication. Dating is complicated at the CIA. Any foreigner you date needs to be reported. And approved.

If only the CIA could have screened some of the bad American women I chose to date!

Photo by Alena Darmel.

41. DIARRHEA IN THE NAME OF DIPLOMACY

During one of my previous trips, I got a little food poisoning.

This is not unusual, as CIA analysts often travel to exotic locales and do not hesitate to integrate into the culture. Often this means eating street food or eating at questionable restaurants.

After getting sick, I found myself on future trips being extra careful with what I ate and drank, to make sure I wouldn't get sick again.

But sometimes, CIA analysts have to get sick, in the name of diplomacy.

Often, CIA analysts would be included in meetings with intelligence services from other countries, to exchange information. Only months after the trip where I got sick, I found myself at one of these meetings in a unique country. The topic was extremely vital to US national security.

I was very careful with my food and drink during the

trip, and I did not get sick at all.

The meetings were going well, too. But then, the intelligence service took us to the room where lunch would be served. To this day, I don't know what food they served us. But the second I saw the dish, I knew it included a side of diarrhea.

> "The second I saw the dish, I knew it included a side of diarrhea."

But I had to eat it. This was diplomacy, after all.

As expected and like clockwork, I awoke at 2 AM with an immediate need to run to the bathroom.

Sure, movies show Jason Bourne risking his life for his country, but the movies never seem to show CIA analysts enduring diarrhea for their country!

To be fair, maybe it's best we don't show this one in the movies…

Artificial Intelligence's attempt at recreating the Real Jack Ryan's sprint to the toilet. (Photo by Dall-E)

42. YOU KNOW THAT GUY YOU JUST OFFERED COCAINE TO? HE'S WITH THE CIA.

While with the CIA, I spent most of my time working with the CIA's Crime and Narcotics Center. That made this New Year's Eve story even more ironic.

That year, I went out to dinner and a party. A pretty standard New Year's Eve. Nothing out of the ordinary.

As I was returning to my apartment building, I ran into a group of friendly people. They were asking me how to find a particular building in the building complex. I helped them, and then they invited me to the party they were going to.

I figured, "Why not?" So I went.

In less than 30 minutes, the host of the party offered me cocaine.

First, there's a certain irony in offering cocaine to any CIA officer, which of course they didn't know I was.

But worse, they were offering cocaine to an officer of

the CIA's Crime and Narcotic's Center!

I politely declined and, soon after, went home.

This did not go into my nose that evening.

43. CIA ANALYST TRAVELING FOR PLEASURE FORGETS TO SECURE A VISA?!

CIA analysts are generally savvy travelers. Our passports, both the fake ones and the real ones, collect a lot of stamps. But even CIA analysts are not above making mistakes when it comes to visas and international travel.

I was in Kyiv, Ukraine, years after I left the Agency and long before the horrible Russian invasion there. I wanted to go to Moscow, next. I had never been to Russia before. So I booked a ticket and reserved lodging in Moscow.

Russia isn't exactly friendly territory. The KGB, now called the FSB, is known to be an aggressive intelligence service. And I had reason to believe that the FSB knew that I was once a CIA officer.

So, to be safe, I gave my parents all of my local information and told them I would message them every day. The idea was that if I didn't message them and they didn't hear from me, something was wrong.

I thought I was preparing wisely!

My flight from Kyiv to Moscow had a layover in Minsk, Belarus. When I was going through customs at Minsk, they asked me, "Do you have a visa to go to Russia?"

> "When I was going through customs at Minsk, they asked me, "Do you have a visa to go to Russia?""

I was shocked; needing a visa never crossed my mind. Typically, Americans can just flash their powerful US tourist passport and they're good to go.

I told them no, I did not have a visa to enter Russia. And they responded by telling me there was no way I was getting on the next plane and no way I could get into Russia.

Fortunately, Belarus had recently passed a law allowing western foreigners to stay something like a week without having a visa in advance. So, unexpectedly, I was now spending a week in Belarus!

I'm pleased with how things turned out. How many people spend time in Minsk? And whereas Moscow has become a cosmopolitan, worldly city, Minsk has not. Minsk is how I envision the Russia of the past being.

Moral of the story, even well-traveled CIA analysts forget that they need a visa, sometimes.

*The Real Jack Ryan in Minsk, Belarus
in front of a statue of Vladimir Lenin and a lone bureaucrat.*

The Real Jack Ryan in Minsk, Belarus.

44. What job do you take after leaving the CIA?

When your first job is the CIA, what are you supposed to do after you leave? They never show that in the movies!

First, I did nothing. I moved to Florida, and the plan was to take a year of "retirement" in Florida, playing volleyball and relaxing on the beach.

Life as a CIA analyst is intense. It's not a natural transition to sit at the beach.

I made it about 6 months before I found myself doing security consulting. The work started with physical security for corporations, and then morphed into physical security for computer systems, which then morphed into cybersecurity.

Consulting was a good gig. I would work maybe one week every couple of months and I would earn enough that week to pay for the other 7 weeks. I found the work rewarding for that one week, but unfortunately I found myself spending those other 7 weeks searching for the next project, which was not the most rewarding.

Fortunately, all of that changed when one of my clients asked me to create a cybersecurity software company with him. We built the company, raised venture capital funding, and grew the company into a multi-million dollar company. The company is called CyberSaint Security.

I also advised another cybersecurity startup based in Ukraine, and owned a portion of that company, which I ultimately sold. It also is a multi-million dollar company that is doing well, called SOC Prime.

> "At the end of the scheduled meetings, they didn't know what to do with me."

At one point, I interviewed with a top home improvement corporation. They flew me to their headquarters and had me meet with 6 different managers. At the end of the scheduled meetings, they didn't know what to do with me, and had me meet with their Director of Strategy, too. In the end, they couldn't find a proper fit and decided not to hire me.

In short, there are not many relevant jobs for someone leaving the CIA. I'm now a tech startup guy. My latest company is a privacy company called ZenPrivata that is backed by venture capital and is growing.

Photo by Robert Nagy.

CHAPTER 8

LESSONS LEARNED: SOME SURPRISING
TAKEAWAYS FROM MY TIME WITH CIA

Working at the CIA, you gain insight into current and past events like few in the world have. You get to know things that almost nobody knows. And as you'll gather from the first story in this chapter, most people don't really know much.

Sadly, most of these insights are classified and I can't share them. However, I was able to find a few that the CIA will allow me to share with you.

Here are some highlights you'll find in this chapter.

45. Most experts are clueless

46. Joseph McCarthy wasn't as crazy as we were taught

47. People are waaaaay too paranoid about the government

45. MOST EXPERTS ARE CLUELESS

After having access to classified information and being one of the few people in the world "in the know" for some time, it was very interesting to observe debates in the media and comments coming from "experts." My realization, experts have absolutely no clue what they are talking about. And that's true on both ends of the political spectrum.

I realized this most starkly when I left the Agency and was setting up meetings with people, deciding what to do next in life. One of these meetings was with Howard Altman from the Tampa Bay Times, and we started discussing the hot topics of the moment. He mentioned one debate, and I was flabbergasted. He said there was an ongoing debate about whether the Mexican drug cartels would smuggle terrorists into the United States. Both sides spoke about and had written many viewpoints that sounded very confident and logical. But that doesn't mean they were true, or even reasonable.

If I hadn't had access to classified information, I might have heard the "experts" argue one of the sides–that the cartels might smuggle a terrorist into the United States, and believed them. I might think that they knew what they were talking about. But in reality, they didn't have a clue.

> "If I hadn't had access to classified
> information, I might have heard the
> "experts" and believed them."

In my opinion, (remember, I've been out of the CIA for 7 years, now), there is nearly zero chance of cartels smuggling terrorists into the USA. About as zero as zero gets. Quite the opposite, actually. If I were a terrorist, I would go out of my way to avoid the cartels, fearing for my life.

But the experts didn't seem to really know what was going on. They just spoke as if they knew what they were talking about.

For this reason, I highly recommend questioning expert opinions, no matter how eloquent or smart the expert is. Always try to read the primary materials— the actual court transcript, the messages sent, the phone records—whatever direct materials are needed to make a judgment on your own. You want to hear it "straight from the horse's mouth". Because the experts are only going to be slightly better than a coin toss when it comes to getting things right.

I ultimately did an interview with the newspaper and an article was published, setting the record straight. Still, even in that article there were rebuttals from the (clueless) experts.

Photo by Sachin Bharti.

46. JOSEPH MCCARTHY WASN'T AS CRAZY AS WE WERE TAUGHT

One topic seems to be universally portrayed and taught the same way. And perhaps incorrectly, I found while I was at the CIA. And that topic is McCarthyism and the Red Scare.

The Red Scare was a period after World War 2 in which many accusations were made that US Government officials and many other people were secretly communists and treasonists.

The period is often referred to as a "Which Hunt," akin to the trials in Salem, Massachusetts in the 1700s when many women were burned at the stake for being witches. The sentiment is that those people that McCarthy and others were calling communists were being treated like the Salem women, and were being "burned" for no reason.

The Red Scare is almost always taught with a negative connotation, and Joseph McCarthy is generally portrayed as a madman. For example, Encyclopedia Britannica—generally an extremely neutral, unbiased source—says that McCarthy "lacked evidence for his claims," which were "increasingly outlandish."

Interestingly, Britannica also notes that McCarthy was particularly critical of President Truman's administration, singling out Secretary of State Dean Acheson, Secretary of Defense George Marshall, and even Truman himself.

Of course, I learned all of this in school and read it all in the history books before joining the CIA.

After joining the CIA, however, I took a class at the The Centre for Counterintelligence and Security Studies to learn more about counterintelligence.

There, I was fortunate enough to meet Oleg Kalugin, the former head of the Soviet Union's Washington DC operations who had since defected to the United States. In that position, Kalugin led all spy operations in Washington targeting the United States. His job was to recruit Americans to give US information to the Soviet Union.

Oleg is a very interesting, smart man. If I'm The Real Jack Ryan, he's the real Spycraft, for those who remember the game from the 90's. The game is based largely on him. I'm honored to have met him and was delighted to pick his brain.

One topic that came to mind that was prevalent during his tenure was, what did he think about Joseph

McCarthy and the Red Scare? Was the reality pretty much the same as what the history books say?

Kalugin's response shocked me. Oleg told me that Joseph McCarthy was generally correct. In fact, Kalugin's officers had even recruited one of Truman's Vice Presidential candidates.

> "Joseph McCarthy was generally correct.
> Soviet intelligence officers had even
> recruited one of Truman's Vice Presidential
> candidates."

Can you imagine if a US Vice President were a Soviet Spy? It may have almost happened. Keep in mind that Truman was a Vice President who became President when Franklin D. Roosevelt died. If that Soviet-controlled Vice President were in office when Truman passed, we could have had a Soviet-controlled President leading the United States.

It's a good lesson. A lot of what we think and generally accept as truth may actually be wrong.

AMERICANS.....
DON'T PATRONIZE REDS!!!!

——•——

YOU CAN DRIVE THE REDS OUT OF TELEVISION, RADIO AND HOLLY-WOOD.....

THIS TRACT WILL TELL YOU HOW.

WHY WE MUST DRIVE THEM OUT:

1) The REDS have made our Screen, Radio and TV Moscow's most effective Fifth Column in America . . . 2) The REDS of Hollywood and Broadway have always been the chief financial support of Communist propaganda in America . . . 3) OUR OWN FILMS, made by RED Producers, Directors, Writers and STARS, are being used by Moscow in ASIA, Africa, the Balkans and throughout Europe to create hatred of America . . . 4) RIGHT NOW films are being made to craftily glorify MARXISM, UNESCO and ONE-WORLDISM . . . **and via your TV Set they are being piped into your Living Room—and are poisoning the minds of your children under your very eyes ! ! !**

So REMEMBER — If you patronize a Film made by RED Producers, Writers, Stars and STUDIOS you are aiding and abetting COMMUNISM .. . . every time you permit REDS to come into your Living Room VIA YOUR TV SET you are helping MOSCOW and the INTERNATIONALISTS to destroy America ! ! !

47. PEOPLE ARE WAAAAAY TOO PARANOID ABOUT THE GOVERNMENT

There is a lot of paranoia about the government and the CIA. I've encountered many people who feared that, once I joined the CIA, that their calls or conversations with me would be listened to, and that they would need to speak carefully.

> "For the most part, no one at CIA or the US Government cares what you do."

To be fair, I did become someone who was scrutinized more than your average person. But the truth is that for the most part, no one at CIA or the US Government cares what you do. Most people just aren't that important. Even while working at the CIA, I could have reported that my uncle had 30 anti-American books, and no one would care much or be concerned.

Is this person really going to act on that anti-Americanism? Do they have plans? Have they organized or mobilized? Is this person truly a threat?

The reality is, there are bigger fish to fry. There are so many more true threats. And limited resources to address them. The US Government does not care enough about Jim Bob Smith to devote resources to investigate him. The reality is that the US Government probably does not care about you enough to listen to your phone conversations. Or the phone conversations of anyone who is paranoid that the US Government is listening to them.

Once you're on the inside, you realize how little attention the government pays to low-threat individuals, and how wrong many of the conspiracy theorists and paranoid people are.

Photo by Rory LNU.

CHAPTER 9

RANDOM QUESTIONS I'M OFTEN ASKED

They say there are no stupid questions. I can say with confidence that this is not true!

However, I am usually happy to answer any question I am asked, so long as I'm able... And I've been asked them all!

This chapter delves into some of the questions I've been asked. Perhaps they're the questions you would ask me, yourself, if we were to sit down and grab a beer.

Here are some highlights you'll find in this chapter.

48. How many countries have you been to? Which is your favorite?

49. Do you still work for the CIA?

50. Do you like any spy movies or shows? Are any realistic? Which is your favorite?

51. Is George W. Bush dumb & President Obama smart?

52. Have you ever killed anyone?

48. HOW MANY COUNTRIES HAVE YOU BEEN TO? WHICH IS YOUR FAVORITE?

29 countries. And honestly, most were from after I was with the CIA.

Argentina
Bahrain
Belarus
Brazil
Canada
Colombia
Czech Republic
Denmark
England
France
Germany
Greece
Holland
Hungary
Italy
Kazakhstan (Where Borat is from)
Kyrgyzstan (Some people think I made this country up, when I tell them!)

Latvia

Mexico

Paraguay

Peru

Poland

Romania

Scotland

Tajikistan

Turkey

Ukraine

United States

Vatican City (Technically a country)

Which country is my favorite is a question that's almost impossible to answer.

Warsaw, Poland was my first foray into living abroad. I chose Warsaw because it was more exotic than West Europe. Places like Berlin and Paris, aside from Paris's unbelievable beauty and tremendous cafe culture, are very similar to the US. But Warsaw was also not too exotic, for my first try at living outside the United States.

In the end, Warsaw was not as exotic as I expected, so I hopped to Ukraine, which was a little more adventurous. I have been to Ukraine twice, and it's a great country to visit. Unfortunately, Vladimir Putin has probably ruined that for a long time.

Colombia and Argentina are great countries to live in.

I have spent a lot of time in Colombia, and there is a reason for that. It's a wonderfully pleasant place with extremely friendly people, a culture not too different from the United States, and good infrastructure and comforts of life. But you definitely need to speak Spanish to appreciate it. Argentina is similar, but with nicer (although decaying) buildings and cities.

I really enjoyed Belarus, mostly because it's so unlike what we're used to. You can go to most any country in the world, and the capital and major cities will be mostly similar to the United States. Or at the very least there will be a touristic zone or a zone where the wealthy and privileged live that will be familiar and similar to what you'll experience anywhere else. In Belarus, not so much.

Which country is my favorite? The question is unanswerable!

Visiting Pripyat, the city in Ukraine that was abandoned because of the Chernobyl nuclear disaster. You're more likely to find me in an abandoned, radioactive pool than at a beach resort.

49. Do you still work for the CIA?

No.

Because of all the traveling I do, people seem to think I'm still doing work for the CIA.

I wish! As an entrepreneur, there are certainly times that a steady government paycheck would have been appreciated.

But no, I have nearly zero contact with the CIA. They only want to hear from me when I write a book or an article, so they can review it.

> "The CIA only wants to hear from me when I write a book or an article, so they can review it."

However, I do miss the work. I would be happy to take on some projects here and there, if anyone at the CIA is reading this!

50. Do you like any spy movies or shows? Are any realistic? Which is your favorite?

For the most part, no. I find spy movies and shows to be horrendously bad, actually, and have had almost no interest in them. And I have found Hollywood to be atrociously inaccurate when portraying anything to do with the CIA or spies.

I have no interest in watching car chases and murders. The real spy game is actually incredibly tedious and meticulous. Imagine driving 30 minutes before meeting with a source just to make absolutely sure no one's following you. That's the reality. But that would make for a pretty boring movie!

> "The reality of spycraft would make for a pretty boring movie!

The reality is more sitting and planning, and being ready for whatever might happen.

The one exception was The Americans, which I thought was phenomenal and mostly realistic. The operations were plausible and their operational security was spot-on.

They cover their tracks. They plan for everything. They try to avoid fights and murders, instead using intelligence and cunning to collect information. And the show is about collecting information, which is what intelligence is really about. The show is very well-done and I highly recommend it. Fair warning, though, the show is about Russian KGB officers posing as Americans.

51. Is George W. Bush dumb & President Obama smart?

We often see President George W Bush portrayed as a bit of a dolt, and President Obama presented as a studious, smarter president.

From these perceptions, you might assume that President Bush was not as intelligent of a reader of the analysis we presented to him in the Presidential Daily Brief (PDB), while President Obama was a voracious, thorough reader of intelligence.

But you would be wrong.

I've written many analyses directly to both presidents, and I can declare with confidence that President Bush was a more thorough reader of PDBs. In fact, when you wrote for President Bush, there was a good chance you'd receive a hand-written note with his comments and follow-up questions.

President Obama, on the other hand, regularly requested shorter, less detailed PDB articles.

This isn't to say that President Obama is not extremely intelligent or that he didn't read the PDB closely. But the differences between the two presidents were stark, and they were not consistent with how the two were presented in the media.

From my interactions with President Bush through the PDB, I think he was misportrayed as a simpler, less intelligent president. And I think he may have just been acting that way because it helped to earn more votes.

52. HAVE YOU EVER KILLED ANYONE?

If I told you, I'd have to kill you!

But seriously no, I've never killed anyone.

Afterword

Thanks so much for reading. I very much enjoyed writing this book and I hope you enjoyed reading it!

If so, please leave a review and tell a friend, as this will help get the book out to more people who may enjoy reading it.

If you have any questions, comments, or would like a sequel, feel free to connect with me and write me on Instagram @ScottSchlimmer

Printed in Great Britain
by Amazon

41871309R00088